STUTTERING: GETTING UNSTUCK

I wish you success!

Cheri Jensen

STUTTERING: GETTING UNSTUCK

How To Interrupt The Moment Of Stuttering
And Gain Control Of Your Speech

Second Edition

A Self-Help Book For Adults

Cheri Jensen
Speech Pathologist

authorHOUSE®

AuthorHouse™
1663 Liberty Drive
Bloomington, IN 47403
www.authorhouse.com
Phone: 1-800-839-8640

First published by AuthorHouse   11/04/2011

ISBN: 978-1-4567-9655-6 (sc)
ISBN: 978-1-4567-9653-2 (ebk)

Library of Congress Control Number: 2011915085

Printed in the United States of America

Contents

Dedication

This book is dedicated to my mom, Catherine Vattendahl Radniecki Jensen (1914-2004), who always believed in me and my work; Bill Jensen (1922-1963), my daddy, who would have been proud of my work; my family and friends who encouraged me; Nick Kirchner, who, as an amazing little first grader, was the start of it all; Julia Butler, my delightful, vivacious student; Andy Smith, my dear reluctant student; and to all of my fluency students. I thank you with all my heart.

Preface

The reason I am writing a second book, is that after publishing my first book, GETTING UNSTUCK, 2010, I realized that very few people could find it, because the subject of the book was not in the main title. To change a book title, one has to write a second book.

Writing a second book gave me the opportunity to revise some of the book and add a major section, which I had wanted to do since my first publication. While writing the first book, I had an inkling that I was onto something new, but it had not jelled at that time. After publishing that book, I became acutely aware of the additional stretch, which I was using much more broadly than I had stated in the book. I began to pay attention to this additional stretch to see how I was using it, and exactly when and how I was using it. After figuring it out, I realized that it was a very effective companion to the original Stretch. Writing a second edition gave me the opportunity to share this new information.

After seeing the movie, "The King's Speech", I was very determined to get this information out to you as soon as possible. Since that movie came out, the subject of stuttering has been coming out of the closet. The timing was very good for a new, effective fluency technique to become available to the public.

Now, just a bit about me and the history of my stuttering, and how I developed my original fluency technique.

When I was a kid, I stuttered. My parents were told that it was best to just ignore it and that it probably would go away. It didn't go away, and no one knew how much it bothered me. Because of my stuttering, I did not gain the self-confidence to thrive at school and I became an underachiever. I dreaded being called on in class, and felt mortified whenever I had to read aloud, because of the hard blocks or repetitions. I wouldn't give spontaneous answers or comments in class for fear of stuttering.

The first time that I read anything about stuttering, I was an undergraduate at Moorhead State University in the Speech Pathology and Audiology program, in 1964. I was 19 years old.

Lonnie Emeric, the grand mogul, as we affectionately called him, was the professor of my first class on stuttering. His hero was Charles Van Riper, and though I learned a lot about stuttering and Van Riper's approaches to fluency, none of his approaches were helpful to me.

My first and only experience receiving speech therapy services for my stuttering was with a graduate student, while I was an undergrad. It was not helpful. After that I was on my own again.

Later on, after I graduated from MSU, I went to work in the public school system in Daytona Beach, Florida. I tried different ways to correct my own stuttering and that of my students. I was not successful. My stuttering was generally considered mild, but I always found my repetitions and hard blocks very embarrassing and sometimes just down right humiliating. My stuttering got in the way of spontaneous communication, during conversations with friends, in groups, in meetings, at parties, ordering certain foods, saying certain names, etc. Those of you who stutter know what I'm talking about. Also, it was very frustrating that there was nothing out there for me nor my students who stuttered.

After moving back to Minnesota, I earned my Master's Degree in Speech Pathology, at Mankato State

University in 1979. In 1980, I went to work in the Stillwater, MN school system, where, in 1988, I met Nick Kirchner, a little first grader, who stuttered severely. I was determined to not fail this child. I began my hunt, again, to find a fluency program/technique that worked. I found a few that could be effective, but they were uncomfortable to practice and not transferable to everyday speech. I came up with different techniques, which were trial and error, and eventually came up with one that was a precursor to the Cheri J. Stretch Technique. Nick was successful with it!

A few years later, while working trial and error again, this time with Julia Butler, my 7th grade student, I discovered that I had come up with a different sort of stretch that helped to *skip over the stutter.* It was *significantly different* than other stretch techniques that I had read about and tried with myself and my students. I realized that what I was teaching Julia and using myself was *different and very effective.* It was easy to learn and use, blended into ones vocal inflections, sounded normal and no one knew it was being used. Thus I developed the Cheri J. Stretch Technique, to help control and reduce stuttering. It was Julia who said, "Write a book about it, Ms, Jensen". She also said that I must use my first name in the technique title, so that people would know that a woman developed it. Thank you for the encouragement, Julia!

Acknowledgement

The first two people who influenced the writing of this book, were my mother, Catherine, and Julia Butler, my first student to use the program. My mom always believed in me and my work, which gave me courage to go forth. My delightful beyond words, vivacious student, Julia Butler, encouraged me to write a book and dedicate it to her. Andy Smith, another seventh grade student, who did not want to go to speech therapy for his stuttering, agreed to give my technique a shot if I dedicated my book to him, also. He liked the technique and was successful with it. Thank you all for your encouragement.

Developing the Cheri J. Stretch Technique actually began 21 years ago, with the little first grader, Nick Kirchner, who stuttered severely. Until that time, I had not successfully dealt with severe stuttering, or any stuttering, for that matter, and I was determined not to fail this child. I was determined to find a way to help him. Thus began my journey to find a fluency technique that worked, which led me to develop the Cheri J. Stretch Technique. Later, during my quest to further control my stuttering, I developed the companion, the Cheri J. Added Stretch.

The people along the way, who gave me encouragement to continue with my stutter program and to write this second edition are: my aunt, Alice Bergeron; my sisters, Judy J. Lindberg, Mary J. Otto and Wendy J. Ryan; my friends, Edie Naomi Smith, Laurie Bauer and Jane Mortenson. Many thanks to you for your support.

A special thanks to my sister, Mary J. Otto, for pointing out the manner in which to rewrite paragraphs, and pull things together in the book, to make better sense of it all, and to make it pleasing to the eye, so that it is easily read. Thank you, Mary.

A special thanks to my sister, Wendy J. Ryan, for helping me come up with the brilliant book cover for the second edition, as well as the first. Her artistic talents and expertise in book publishing were invaluable. Thank you, Wendy.

A special thanks to my friend, Jane Mortenson, for editing my second edition. Her expertise, experience and excellent eye were greatly appreciated. Thank you, Jane.

A special thanks to my friend, Laurie Bauer, for editing my second edition as well as my first book, *GETTING UNSTUCK.* Laurie's encouragement and suggestions for my first book gave me the courage to write the second edition. She read the second edition as a consumer as well as a speech pathologist. Her comments and editing were much appreciated. Thank you, Laurie.

With deepest gratitude,
Cheri Jensen

About The Author

Cheri Jensen, BS, MS, is a retired Speech Pathologist, from the Stillwater school district, in Minnesota, where she worked for 28 years. Prior to that, she worked in the Daytona Beach, Florida school system for nine years and in Waseca, Minnesota for one year. The area of stuttering has been her focus since 1988. Since Cheri also stutters, she had a special interest in finding techniques that decreased stuttering and also gave those who stuttered more control over their speech. The Cheri J. Stretch Technique, to help control and reduce stuttering, was developed out of her great concern for her students who stuttered. It was her hope that her technique would help them gain control over their stuttering, thus making a positive difference in their lives.

Cheri practiced using her technique while teaching her students to use it. After three years of use, her fluency technique became a natural part of her speech, reduced her stuttering and gave her more control over her speech.

After retiring from the Stillwater, MN school district, Cheri realized that she wanted to share her fluency technique with other adults who stutter. She wrote the book, *GETTING UNSTUCK.*

After recently developing a companion stretch, which she found very useful in further controlling and reducing stuttering, she knew that she needed to write a second book. So she wrote a second edition, *STUTTERING: GETTING UNSTUCK.*

Purpose

The purpose of this book is to aid those who stutter, to increase the possibility of taking charge of their own speech, by gaining control of their stuttering, reducing the frequency of their stuttering, thus gaining more fluency and more confidence in speaking.

THE CHERI J. STRETCH AND THE CHERI J. ADDED STRETCH:

Techniques For Fluency
To Help Control And Reduce Stuttering

INTRODUCTION

So you stutter. Chances are that you will always stutter. These are the facts, plain and simple. However, I believe that with the Cheri J. Stretch Techniques for Fluency Program, you quite possibly could learn to control most, or all of your stuttering and, over time, reduce the frequency of stuttering—possibly significantly. I did well with the original *Cheri J. Stretch Technique* for about ten years.

When I developed the *companion* stretch, the *Cheri J. Added Stretch,* I was very excited with the results. It was easy to use, it made talking easier and my fluency increased. The combination of the two stretches were so effective, I knew that I had to write a second edition of my first book, *GETTING UNSTUCK*. I wanted you to have the same opportunity to increase your chances of success.

WHO STUTTERS?

I stutter. More males stutter than females, but so what? Whether you are male or female, if you stutter, you stutter. Many people stutter. Some are famous and many are not. Some are wealthy, some are poor, and many are in between. Some are highly intelligent and some not so much. People of all nationalities and from all countries stutter. As you can see, you are not alone.

WHAT CAUSES STUTTERING?

This question has baffled speech pathologists and scientists for centuries—yes—centuries. It is believed that Moses and Aristotle stuttered. We do know that it tends to run in families and that stress is involved. That's about all we really know for sure.

Barry Guitar said, in his book, *Stuttering, An Integrated Approach to Its Nature and Treatment, Second Edition* (1999), "Exactly what neural organizations predispose a person to stuttering are not known. What is known is that there are many contributing factors to stuttering."

Charles Van Riper, speech pathologist, researcher, author and one who stuttered, worked his whole life on the cause and "cure" for stuttering. He believed that stuttering is complex and multidimensional, a belief held by many current speech pathologists and researchers/authors. He worked with thousands of people who stuttered, and stated that none of his therapy techniques had any lasting effects. At some point, he realized that there is no "cure" for stuttering, per se, but to have lasting improvements, those who stutter need to change their attitudes toward stuttering and themselves, from self-loathing to acceptance. My program addresses this.

Martin Schwartz, another authority in the area of stuttering, who developed a very effective but cumbersome fluency technique, stated that stress is indeed involved in stuttering, and stress that targets the vocal cords is the main culprit. Both of the Cheri J. Stretches target stress to the vocal cords, and are very effective in reducing it.

Marty Jezer, a gifted writer and one who stutters severely, wrote a wonderful non-technical book, *Stuttering: A Life Bound Up In Words*. It is one of the most informative and humorous books that I have read on the subject of stuttering. Marty is deeply honest about his stuttering experiences, and wrote from his heart. I highly recommend reading his book.

OF THE MANY THEORIES REGARDING THE POSSIBLE CAUSES OF STUTTERING, THE FOLLOWING MAKES THE MOST SENSE TO ME:

Some researchers in the area of stuttering believe that those who stutter may have, as a predisposition to stuttering, a slight deficiency in the region of the brain that processes hearing, thus creating a slight delay in hearing what *oneself* has just said. These disruptions, though slight, cause some confusion during the speaking process, resulting in involuntary speech disruptions, which create frustration and embarrassment in the child, who is just learning to speak. As the child's speech and language continue to expand, these speech mishaps and the struggle to speak continues. Then embarrassment is added to the mix. As time goes on, feelings of ineptitude are added. As the involuntary speech disruptions continue, and the feelings of frustration, embarrassment, humiliation and ineptitude are fully established, the speech disruptions, along with the negative emotions attached to them, lock into the child's memory.

Initially, these emotions are not the cause of stuttering. The speech disruptions cause these emotions. Shame, humiliation, anxiety, fear of talking and embarrassment become attached to the speech disruptions, because of the difficulty in getting the words out and thinking that everyone is judging you. Over time, as the intensity of the emotions increase, these involuntary speech disruptions, the struggle to control them, plus the feelings of frustration, embarrassment, humiliation and ineptitude regarding the disruptions, become a self-perpetuating vicious cycle and develop into what has been termed, "stuttering." *Eventually, emotions do indeed cause the stuttering, because they become the stutter trigger.* The vicious cycle continues.

Whether the stuttering is severe or mild, the one who stutters feels shamed and humiliated. The shame and humiliation of stuttering too often become the shame of oneself.

Stuttering sometimes becomes a family secret, whether the stuttering is mild or severe, frequent or infrequent, or whether much of it is hidden or very obvious. It becomes the ELEPHANT IN THE LIVING ROOM, with everyone walking around it, pretending that it does not exist. This is not healthy and it adds to the shame, humiliation, etc. of stuttering.

Children who stutter can become underachievers. Sometimes the children who stutter are bullied by parents, siblings and other children. This, of course, creates greater anxiety, shame, humiliation, etc. and more stuttering.

As these children grow into adults, some do not meet their full potential, and go into professions in which they feel the most secure—not necessarily the professions they would truly like to have. Others are in professions in which they are truly qualified and enjoy, but their stuttering still interferes with communication.

THE STUTTERING

CORE BEHAVIORS

For those who stutter, one size does not fit all. Some stutter mildly, some severely and many in between. Also, there are many types of stutter behaviors, called core behaviors. In case you are interested, Barry Guitar adopted the term, "core behaviors," from Van Riper, who used it to describe the basic, involuntary behaviors of stuttering: REPETITIONS, PROLONGATIONS AND BLOCKS.

DO YOU SEE YOURSELF in one or more of the following descriptions?

REPETITIONS: You pretty much know what these are. They are the "ddddo yyyyou wwwwant to dddance?"

"He-he-he-he is coming over tonight." "She danced beau-beau-beau-beau beautifully." I was an expert at this one.

BLOCKS: Being "stuck" on a word—holding on to the first sound (k, b, p, t, etc.)—holding your breath—lips or tongue locked in place—can't get the word out. This is very familiar to me.

PROLONGATIONS: While you are in the process of saying (vocalizing) a word, you *uncontrollably* string out a word by holding onto a sound (phoneme) way too long. It is an *uncontrolled* stretch. The prolongation may be in the beginning or middle of a word.

AVOIDANCE OF STUTTERING THAT CAN BECOME THE STUTTERING

Most people who stutter, do not want to stutter, and some will do almost anything to not stutter, so they develop avoidance behaviors. However, most of the behaviors used to avoid stuttering are very distracting to the listener and interfere with communication. The most common behaviors used to avoid stuttering are:

COPIOUS INTERJECTIONS: an example is "Um, um, um, um, she is um, um, um, not home." When a long string of *ums* or *ands*, etc. are used as an attempt to not stutter, they become the stuttering.

SECONDARY BEHAVIORS: peculiar head movements, body movements, tongue clicking, snorting, etc., used as avoidance behaviors to prevent stuttering on a particular word, and to help "get the word out". These behaviors are just as distracting to the listener as actual core stuttering, but the one using these behaviors is oblivious to it. S/he believes that what s/he is doing to not stutter looks or sounds just fine, and that it is a great substitute for the stuttering. These behaviors become the stuttering!

SITUATION AND WORD AVOIDANCE: hiding one's stuttering, by not speaking when wanting to; omitting stutter words; avoiding certain people; not ordering certain foods; often not asking question; etc., etc. Situation and word avoidance do not become the stuttering. They interfere with one's communication, cause misery and exhaustion, and often limit one's quality of communication, and possibly quality of life.

WHAT DO WE DO ABOUT IT?!

THE FOLLOWING ARE A FEW STEPS TO TAKE BEFORE STARTING PRACTICE WITH THE STRETCH TECHNIQUES:

AN IMPORTANT FIRST STEP in doing something about stuttering, is to realize that most, if not all, people have some dysfluencies, some of which sound like stuttering and some not. The point is that some dysfluency is natural. Listen to people who do not stutter. Listen to how they speak. What is it that they do that sounds like stuttering? They add *ums*; use extra *ands*; repeat the first word of their sentence; stop and start over; hesitate; and revise their sentences. Some even make stutter sounding repetitions, as in *cccookies.*

Yes, I know that stuttering is very different than general dysfluency. So why am I telling you about it? I want you to know that dysfluency is the norm, not the exception. I believe it is helpful to know this.

SECOND, PUT STUTTERING IN ITS PLACE. Realize that it is not a character flaw. It is a PROBLEM THAT DISRUPTS COMMUNICATION, which is a major pain in the tush. And of course the shame and humiliation of it, that we have developed over the years, is not to be taken lightly. Nor can the anguish that it has caused. IT IS NOT, HOWEVER, A CHARACTER FLAW.

THE THIRD STEP IS A BIG ONE: *working on getting rid of the elephant in the living room.* You KNOW that it exists, but you, as well as everyone else, walks around it, keeping it a big secret. Heaven forbid that anyone would talk about it. Yes, even the one who stutters wants to pretend it is not there. Well, it is. It just is.

How do we get rid of the elephant? The first step, and a really big one, is to make PEACE with your stuttering i.e. desensitize the negative feelings about stuttering. Stuttering needs to be "de-awfulized" as Bill Murray, speech pathologist and stutter authority, coined many years ago. You start by admitting to yourself, aloud, that you stutter. Get used to the word. Say it a lot. Say, "I stutter, I stutter, I stutter". Maybe write it several times on a piece of paper. Get comfortable with it. You could use a euphemism, a word or expression that you think is less unpleasant, but other people will call it stuttering. So you may as well, too. I believe that it is a major step in desensitizing, especially for adults.

HOWEVER, SOME OF YOU JUST CANNOT AND WILL NOT USE THE WORD, "STUTTER". It has caused too much pain. You may want to call it "Stammering." Or "My speech disorder." Or "My speech thing." Or whatever. That's OK. It really is. THE IMPORTANT THING IS TO ACKNOWLEDGE IT, SO THAT IT CAN BE DESENSITIZED.

After you get comfortable with hearing yourself say, "I stutter" (or whatever you have decided to call it—I will use the word "stutter" for simplification), you will be ready for the next step, which is also a big one. THE FOURTH STEP IS TO BE OPEN ABOUT YOUR STUTTERING. No, not to the whole world. Heavens! At first, find one trusted person with whom you feel comfortable, with whom you can talk about your stuttering. You might simply say, "Yes, I stutter." You might give the history of your stuttering. You might share this book. Whatever you feel comfortable with. You tell ONLY those you *trust*, and you certainly don't have to tell everyone you know. That is totally up to you. This process helps to further desensitize the negative feelings wrapped around stuttering, and helps you to start rebuilding your self-esteem and confidence.

Telling another person that you stutter is a big step, so give yourself a lot of praise for doing so!

Telling others that I stutter was a difficult step for me, even as a speech pathologist, working with students who stutter! As I began using my technique a lot, and was gaining much more fluency than I had ever had, I still felt shame and humiliation. It occurred to me that I was still keeping my stuttering a "secret." I realized that I needed to name it and talk about it. First, I started by talking openly to my fluency students, telling them my story of stuttering. Then I opened up to their parents, telling my story, explaining the fluency technique, how it has helped me, and how it was helping their child. After I decided to write a book about about my fluency technique, I opened up to my sisters, my mom and some friends, while telling them about the Stretch technique and my plan to write a book about it. It took me a couple of years, at least, to start feeling comfortable with telling others that I stutter. It has gotten easier over the years.

To be perfectly honest, some of my moments of stuttering continue to be an embarrassment to me. However, telling others that I stutter has truly helped to desensitize much of the negative feeling wrapped around the fact that I stutter. *Bit by little bit, the embarrassment of stuttering has been diminishing.*

So, you see, I know first hand that it is a difficult and important step to tell others that you stutter. The shame and humiliation need to be diminished—melted away. THE ELEPHANT NEEDS TO GO BACK TO AFRICA!

Also, I believe that it is very important to NOT refer to yourself, or anyone else who stutters, as a "stutterer." It is not your identity. It is not who you are. It is what you do. You are a person who stutters.

THE FINAL STEP IS TO FIGURE OUT WHAT IT IS THAT *YOU* DO THAT IS *YOUR* STUTTERING.

DO YOU:

- REPEAT?

- HAVE HARD BLOCKS?

- HAVE UNCONTROLLED PROLONGATIONS?

- USE COPIOUS INTERJECTIONS?

- USE SECONDARY BEHAVIORS?

- AVOID CERTAIN WORDS?

- AVOID CERTAIN SPEAKING SITUATIONS?

- ONE OR MORE OF THE ABOVE?

- SOME OF EACH?

HOW DO I FIGURE THIS OUT?

IF YOU ARE NOT CERTAIN ABOUT WHAT YOUR STUTTER BEHAVIORS ARE:

1. Record a few conversations, then listen to them. Listen for repetitions, prolongations, blocks and/ or copious interjections. This is an excellent way to become aware of your stutter behaviors. The conversations need to be with other people, not with yourself. We don't stutter when we talk to ourselves.

2. Have a few conversations with various friends near a mirror or in front of a video cam, so that you can observe yourself, to see if you are using secondary behaviors.

3. If you are comfortable doing so, ask a trusted friend what stutter behaviors s/he hears or observes.

4. Pay attention to your speech while you are talking, and see what it is that *you* do that is *your* stuttering.

AFTER YOU FIGURE OUT WHAT YOUR STUTTER BEHAVIORS ARE, PAY ATTENTION TO WHEN THEY HAPPEN. DO YOU STUTTER DURING:

- the first sound of a word, regardless of where it occurs in a sentence?

- the first sound of the first word of what you want to say?

- question words: who, what, when, where, how, do you, are you, etc.?

- words beginning with just certain sounds?

- only particular words?

- only in certain situations?

- only with certain people?

- generally all of the time, in most situations?

- other?

It is important to figure out just *what it is that you do that is your stuttering.* This takes much of the *mystery* out of it. Knowledge is power. You will realize that stuttering is not some monster that possesses you. You will realize that STUTTERING IS A BEHAVIOR. BEHAVIORS CAN BE CHANGED OR MODIFIED.

INTRODUCTION TO THE CHERI J. STRETCH AND ITS COMPANION, THE CHERI J. ADDED STRETCH

The FOCUS of this fluency program is to help you gain as much control of your speech as possible, in order to be fluent enough to make communication easier. Complete fluency is not the goal, nor should it ever be. You could very well gain so much fluency that no one knows that you stutter, not that it matters if they do. Well, it actually does matter. It matters a lot. The point is that no matter how good the fluency technique is, as adults, we will probably always stutter. This is not to discourage you, but to tell you the reality of it. It is just that the stutter trigger/response still exists. It will weaken with time, but it never seems to totally go away. However, you could still gain an enormous amount of fluency. I'm telling you this so that you will not be discouraged if, at times, the techniques do not work.

The MAIN OUTCOME of using the CHERI J. STRETCH and its companion, the CHERI J. ADDED STRETCH, is the *interruption* of the *moment of stuttering.* The Cheri J. Stretch helps one to actually SKIP over the stutter, which consequently gives one controlled fluency (the listener thinks you are not stuttering). The Cheri J. Added Stretch helps one to calm the stutter response in the middle of your utterance, before you get to the stutter word, thus nipping it in the bud.

An AMAZING BY-PRODUCT of both *skipping over the stutter,* and *nipping it in the bud*, thus gaining controlled fluency, is that, over time and with lots and lots of practice and use of the combination of both stretches, the percentage of stuttering diminishes, resulting in the reduction of stutter triggers and stutter memory.

As you become more fluent (controlled stuttering), the fear of stuttering in certain situations and with certain people whittles down, bit by bit. You then become more self-confident in even more speaking situations.

After just a short time, when you use the Stretch and the companion, Added Stretch in real-life situations, you will realize the magic they have, even if you feel on display at the time. You will eventually realize that you are the only person who knows that you are using the techniques! All that the listener hears is fluency!

Eventually, you will become accustomed to using the Stretch and the Added Stretch and they will become a natural part of your speech.

KEEP IN MIND THAT THIS TAKES *TIME.*

The techniques are simple and can be used immediately, but the stutter habits are strong and can easily take over. *Overall success is achieved bit by bit, not all at once.*

These stretches do NOT become another way of stuttering. They *facilitate* the control of stuttering and the gaining of fluency.

It is very important to know that any new fluency technique is very scary to use, at first. This is typical when one is learning something new. As you begin this program, you possibly will feel afraid, self-conscious, conspicuous, embarrassed, etc. You more than likely will at least feel awkward. This is normal. Don't sweat it and DON'T let it stop you.

*IT TAKES COURAGE TO MAKE CHANGES,
NO MATTER HOW MUCH ONE WANTS TO MAKE
THOSE CHANGES.*

IN SUMMARY, THE ADVANTAGES of the Cheri J. Stretch Along with the Cheri J. Added Stretch are:

- They help you to actually "skip over the stutter".

- They reduce the percentage of stutter responses.

- They are easy to use.

- They can be used almost immediately.

- They become built into the speaker's verbal inflections, so that it sounds natural.

- They are generally unnoticed by the listener.

- They are used only as needed to control a stutter, after the techniques are mastered.

LET'S BEGIN WITH THE CHERI J. STRETCH TECHNIQUE

This is where the fun begins. Kinda. OK. Work. Yes, this is where the work begins. Well, not so much work as persistence.

The MAGIC that I discovered was to stretch (just a bit) the first VOWEL OF THE FIRST SYLLABLE OF THE STUTTER WORD *while saying the word*. Not the first sound or letter—the first "vowel." Focus on stretching the first vowel and slide into the word. By stretching the first vowel of the first syllable of the stutter word, one *distracts and relaxes the stutter response mechanism, thus skipping over the stutter,* and fluently saying the word. THIS IS THE MAGIC OF THE CHERI J. STRETCH. This is the KEY to the success of my stretch technique, because we usually GET STUCK on the first letter or sound of the first syllable of one's stutter word. That is why it works to focus the stretch on the first vowel of the first syllable of the word, while saying the stutter word.

After practicing, and you BEGIN USING THE STRETCH IN REAL-LIFE SITUATIONS, YOU WILL *FEEL* THE RELEASE OF THE STUTTER RESPONSE MECHANISM. It is very exciting the first time it happens. This experience will encourage you to use the Stretch again and again. As you successfully use the Stretch, and *feel the release of the stutter response mechanism*, the brain starts to make changes. The stutter response mechanism, slowly but surely, becomes triggered less often. This is how, over time, one reduces one's stuttering.

THE STRETCH

The Stretch is a controlled holding on, just a bit, to the vocalization of the first *vowel* of the first syllable of the word. It is done by saying the first sound/letter of the word, but FOCUSING on a vocalized stretch of the FIRST VOWEL of the word. While stretching (vocalizing) the vowel just a bit, use your diaphragm to give a little push, *feel the release of the stutter, then slide into the rest of the word.*

These procedures distract and relax the stutter response, and is how one skips over the stutter.

It will make more sense to you after you start using the Stretch in real-life situations, and EXPERIENCE THE *FEELING* of the *release* of the stutter response.

Example: If the stutter word is *"candle,"* you would say it like this: *caaandle.* Another example: If the stutter word is *"where"*, you would say it like this: *Whehhhre.* Can you see that you vocalize (say) the first sound of the word, *but hold on to the vowel just a bit*, then finish the word?

More examples: If the stutter word is *"remember,"* you would say it like this: *Reeemember.* If the stutter word is *"China,"* you would say it like this: *Chiiina.* If the stutter word is *"computer,"* you would say it like this: *cohhhmputer.*

HERE WE GO! Start your practice program by using the Stretch on single words to get the hang of it. Remember, stretch the first vowel (not the first sound/letter) of the first syllable of each word, feel the release of the stutter response, then slide into the rest of the word, with a little push of the diaphragm It will sound exaggerated. It will be at first. That's OK.

Stay on this level until you feel comfortable with the technique.

SINGLE WORD PRACTICE

SINGLE WORD EXAMPLES:

reeemember (remember)   cohhhmpany (company)

toooday (today)   spahhhghetti (spaghetti)

tooomorrow (tomorrow)   fehhhbruary (February)

beeegin (begin)   greeeen (green)

cohhhmputer (computer)   wiiiindow (window)

myyyyyy (my)   ehhhhlephant (elephant)

stooorm (storm)   kihhhndergarten (kindergarten)

Iiii (I)   cahhhhlendar (calendar)

heee (he)   bihhhrthday (birthday)

sheee (she)   cohhhkies (cookies)

uhhhnder (under)   diiiictionary (dictionary)

eeelection (election)   Mahhhrch (March)

aaattitude (attitude)   Aaaapril (April)

ahhhpologize (apologize) cohhhnstruction (construction)

iiiice cream (ice cream) dehhhhcorations (decorations)

boooat (boat) cohhhntagious (contagious)

peeeches (peaches) reeeefrigerator (refrigerator)

puuumpkin (pumpkin) reeesponsible

raaabit (rabbit) brehhhakfast (breakfast)

reeealize (realize) youuuuu (you)

Jaaanuary (January) graaaduation (graduation)

NOW, YOU make a list of single words to practice, including your typical stutter words, and words starting with your most difficult sounds. Remember, practice stretching the first *vowel*, not the first letter/sound of each word. It will sound exaggerated and probably will be. That's OK. Not to worry. Most of your practice, throughout this program, will sound exaggerated to you and probably to your listeners, but as you learn to use the Stretch in real-life situations, the exaggeration diminishes and it eventually becomes a natural sounding part of your speech inflection.

MAJOR STUTTER CULPRIT

BEFORE WE GO ON TO FURTHER PRACTICE, a MAJOR STUTTER CULPRIT needs to be addressed. *Getting started* is one of our biggest problems. Most of us know that we generally tend to stutter on the first word of what we want to say. Not wanting this to happen, too often we do not say what we want to say, when we want to say it. Sometimes we say nothing. Sometimes we interrupt people by blurting out what we want to say. It truly hampers our communication and is very frustrating. This is where the Cheri J. Stretch works best. It gets us unstuck, so we can get started with what we want to say, when we want to say it, without blurting or speaking out of turn.

Therefore, the following practice of stretching the first vowel of the first syllable of the first word of phrases and sentences is very important.

What I discovered by stretching the first vowel of the first syllable of the first word of my utterance, during real-life communication, was that besides skipping over the stutter, and relaxing the stutter response mechanism, thus beginning my utterance stutter free, I very often created fluency for the rest of the sentence. Cool, huh?

PHRASE PRACTICE

Practice stretching the "first VOWEL" of the first syllable of the first word in the following phrases.

EXAMPLES:

a<u>aa</u>fter (after) we get back

b<u>eee</u>fore (before) the sun goes down

the<u>hhh</u> (the) dice

pl<u>eee</u>se (please) don't

MORE EXAMPLES—Practice stretching the first vowel of the first syllable of the first word of the following phrases:

the danger	before bedtime
in Denmark	by tomorrow
broken dial	last December
it's broken	last year
chocolate shake	next month
vanilla malt	to town
strawberry shortcake	you decide
African American	some toast
I'm Chinese	green frogs
in the dark	Greg is

let's run	pretty shirt
her daughter	remember me
berry bushes	elephant herd
blueberry pie	funny movie
cherry pie	ground hog
sand castle	heavy bag
Judge Judy	North Shore
candy cane	Nebraska is
car cover	Oprah show
kite runner	orange shirt
lemon pie	purple shirt
loud band	pencil sharpener
many presents	quick stop
mountain top	quiet please
Renay Smith	tomorrow night
river bank	Thomas avenue
snowy day	very good

SENTENCE LEVEL
THE OFTEN DREADED,
"QUESTION" SENTENCES

I frequently got stuck on question sentences, and could not participate in conversations, at work during meetings and in other group settings. It was always very frustrating. One day during a meeting at work, when I needed to ask a question and knew I couldn't get started, I found the courage to use the Stretch. It worked! I felt the relaxation of the stutter response! I skipped over the stutter! I was able to ask the question. It was amazing! Exciting! I had been using the Stretch while talking on the phone, talking with my students, and in a few other situations, but never in a group of my colleagues.

QUESTION PRACTICE

Wh<u>ehhh</u>re (where) have you been?

Wh<u>ehhh</u>re (where) did you put it?

Wh<u>ahhh</u>t (what) time is it?

Wh<u>ahhh</u>t (what) do you want to do?

Wh<u>ehhh</u>n (when) did you get back?

Wh<u>ehhh</u>n (when) do you work?

Wh<u>ooo (who)</u> won the game?

Wh<u>ooo</u> (who) is responsible?

H<u>owww</u> (how) much is that?

H<u>owww</u> (how) will you get it done?

D<u>ii</u>id (did) you clean your room?

D<u>ii</u>id (did) you do your homework?

D<u>uhhh</u>se (does) your teacher know about it?

D<u>uhhh</u>se (does) it hurt?

<u>Ii</u>is (is) she finished?

<u>Ii</u>is (is) that yours?

H<u>aaaa</u>s (has) he read the book?

H<u>aaa</u>s (has) she finished her work?

D<u>ooo</u> (do) you want to go?

D<u>ooo</u> (do) you have any more?

A<u>ahh</u>re (are) you hungry?

A<u>ahh</u>re (are) they coming in?

Wh<u>yyyyy</u> (why) are snowflakes white?

Wh<u>yyy</u> (why) did the chicken cross the road?

W<u>iii</u>ll (will) you be on time?

Wiiill (will) they get paid?

Waahhs (was) it your turn?

Waahhs (was) she hired?

Whooo (who) is coming with us?

Dooo (do) you want to join us?

Haauw (how) do we get there?

Whehhhre (where) in Minnesota do you live?

Whahhht (what) are we having for dinner?

Whehhhre (where) are you going?

IIIs it time to go?

Whehhhhre is the best place to get pizza?

THE CHERI J. ADDED STRETCH
(The Companion Stretch)

The Cheri J. Stretch is used the same way on stutter words in the middle of phrases and sentences as it is at the beginning of your utterances. HOWEVER, sometimes, maybe often, during conversations, the Stretch just won't happen. You can't get to it. This is where the ADDED STRETCH comes in. The Added Stretch is simply stretching a vowel of any <u>non</u>-stutter word, *prior* to the stutter word that you feel coming on. I discovered that by stretching a vowel of a non-stutter word or two before I got to the feared stutter word, I could relax the stutter response, and say the stutter word fluently, or at least be able to use the Stretch. The Added Stretch is very effective when used on a non-stutter word right next to the stutter word, but *there are no definite rules regarding which non-stutter word(s) to stretch.*

34

It was my *long-time experience* with *relaxing the stutter response* while using the Stretch, that led me to the Added Stretch. Because of this long-time experience of *feeling* the relaxation of the stutter response, I was able to transfer that feeling to the Added Stretch, thus using it as a fluency technique, along with the Stretch.

THIS IS HOW YOU USE THE ADDED STRETCH: When you have a particularly difficult word coming up, stop, relax, breathe, and start over if needed. Whether or not you start over, slow your speech down just a bit, and stretch a vowel of a non-stutter word or two *prior* to the stutter word, to RELAX THE STUTTER RESPONSE. After you *feel* the relaxation of the stutter response, go ahead and say the stutter word, stutter free. You might also need to use your diaphragm to give the stutter word a little push.

The Added Stretch is particularly useful for REALLY LONG WORDS, and LONG COMBINATIONS OF WORDS (the name of a company, program, etc.). It is used the same way as described above. When you know that a certain long, feared word is coming up, such as *"intravascular"* or *"meteorological,"* or a long combination of words, such as *"Labor and Industrial,"* or *"South Minneapolis Chiropractic Clinic"* start stretching a vowel, just a bit, on non-stutter words *prior* to the feared word(s). Stretch as many non-stutter words as needed, to relax the stutter response. Also, if needed, stretch more than one vowel of the really long stutter words or long—combination stutter words.

In time, as you use the Added Stretch in this way, along with the original
Stretch, you will know which words to stretch and when to stretch them. It will become a regular part of your speech.

I have been using the Added Stretch on a regular basis, during conversations, in combination with the Stretch. The combination of the two stretches has been very effective in keeping the stutter response at bay. It is particularly helpful on days when I am tired or stressed. The Stretch gets me started and the Added Stretch keeps me going.

THE FOLLOWING ARE EXAMPLES OF STRETCHING NON-STUTTER WORDS BEFORE THE STUTTER WORD:

If you know that you will stutter on a feared word, like *"remember,"* you could say,
"D<u>ooo</u> y<u>ouuu</u> remember where to go?"
"Do y<u>ouuu</u> r<u>eee</u>member where to go?"
"D<u>ooo</u> you r<u>eee</u>member?"

If the feared word is "Gary," you could say.

"Iiiis Gary going with us?"
"Iiiis Gaaary going with us?"

More examples, the feared word listed separately

potatoes

Maaay we please haaave potatoes for supper?
Maaay we pleeease have potatoes for supper?
Maaay we please haaave potatoes for supper?
Maaay we please haaave pohhhtatoes for supper?

chocolate malt

III would liiike chocolate malt, please.
III would liiiike a chahhhcolate malt, please.

vanilla

Maaay I have aaah vanilla ice cream cone, please?
Maaay I haaave a vaaanilla ice cream cone please?

Canada

Thehhh (the) farthest I've traveled away from myyyy home iiiis Canada.
Thehhh (the) farthest I've traveled away from my home iiiiis Caaanada.

Italian

Th<u>ehhh</u> languages I can speak are Spanish <u>aaaa</u>nd Italian.
Th<u>ehhh</u> languages I can speak <u>ahhh</u>re (are) Spanish and <u>Iiii</u>talin.

Examples of sentences containing really long words and long combinations of words:

<u>Iii</u> work wiiith <u>Laaa</u>bor and Ind<u>uhhh</u>strial R<u>eee</u>lations.
(I work with Labor and Industrial Relations.)

I need t<u>ooo</u> call C<u>ohhh</u>hmmunity Educ<u>aaa</u>tion to get th<u>ehhh</u> <u>ii</u>information.
(I need to call Community Education to get the information.)

Wh<u>ehhh</u>re is th<u>ehh</u> D<u>eee</u>epartment of Safety <u>aaa</u>nd Insp<u>ehhh</u>ctions located?
(Where is the Department of Safety and Inspections located?)

To find out, g<u>ohhh</u> to th<u>ehhh</u> Office <u>ohhh</u>f T<u>ehhh</u>chnology and Comm<u>uuuu</u>nications in Saint Paul.
(To find out, go the the Office of Technology and Communications in Saint Paul.)

Wh<u>ehhh</u>re can I find th<u>ehhh</u> S<u>ohhh</u>uthwest Corridor Superv<u>iiii</u>sor?
(Where can I find the Southwest Corridor Supervisor?)

** All of the lists of single words, phrases and sentences were selected randomly.

** At any time during your practice program, please feel free to email me with questions, concerns or comments. My email address is on the last page.

BACKUP TECHNIQUE

Certain tough words may persist, especially early in the program, for which the Stretch and the Added Stretch just do not work. It is good to have a backup technique, especially when beginning the fluency program.

THE MARTIN F. SCHWARTZ AIRFLOW TECHNIQUE is an excellent back up technique. What you do is breathe through your nose before saying the stutter word; then, while the throat muscles are relaxed and open, say the word. This is a very good fluency technique, but it tends be very cumbersome, slow and obvious. But it can be a darn good backup and/or additional technique.

At first I used M.F. Schwartz (breathe through your nose before saying the stutter word) quite often, for my really hard words, when I just couldn't get to the Stretch. This was before I came up with the Added Stretch. Now I use it once in a blue moon.

NOW YOU ARE READY TO PRACTICE THE CHERI J. STRETCHES IN REAL-LIFE SITUATIONS

YES, YOU ARE READY. Choose some safe situations for practicing the Cheri J. Stretch. This is the only way you will know the true magic of using it. EXPERIENCE THE MAGIC OF THE *STRETCH* ON A REGULAR BASIS BEFORE ADDING THE *ADDED STRETCH.* It is crucial to truly know how it *feels* to relax the stutter response and skip over the stutter.

After you have had experience with how it *feels* to relax the stutter response, you can then *transfer this feeling to the Added Stretch.* As you stretch a vowel on a non-stutter word, before a stutter word, you will recognize and feel the relaxation of the stutter response of the stutter word coming up, and be able to say that word stutter free.

A GOOD PLACE TO START USING THE CHERI J. STRETCH is to call a store and ask a question. This gives you practice using the technique in public. Practice stretching the first vowel of the first word of what you say, even if you think you won't stutter on the first word. Remember, during ongoing conversations, the first word of what you want to say is often where you get stuck.

When you first start practicing, you will probably feel self-conscious, foolish, conspicuous, etc. This is typical and to be expected. After all, this is really quite new to you. Your listener may notice, but won't dwell on it, because it will be in the realm of normal speech. Remember when I said that it blends into your natural speech inflections? It does. Rest assured that you will NOT make a fool of yourself. Call a couple more stores. Follow the same routine. As you see how well it works, you will want to use the Stretch in other situations.

The trick in being successful with the Stretch is to practice using it all of the time. You may not always be successful, but you will get better with time. Practice every day, several times per day, in different situations.

THIS PART OF THE PROGRAM TAKES COURAGE. You bet it does. Know that you can do it. Be very proud of yourself as you journey forth.

REMEMBER, *it takes courage to make changes, no matter how much one wants those changes.*

HERE ARE FEW MORE SUGGESTED SITUATIONS IN WHICH TO PRACTICE USING THE STRETCH:

- Give your name over the phone.

- Ask a store clerk about an item.

- Phone a store to ask price, information, directions, store hours, etc.

- Introduce one person to another.

- Introduce yourself to someone.

- Order in a restaurant.

- Leave a phone message for someone.

- Telephone to make an appointment.

- Telephone a friend to arrange to get together.

- Read aloud to someone

ADDING THE COMPANION, "ADDED STRETCH" TO YOUR PRACTICE

After you have mastered the Cheri J. Stretch and have experienced the *feeling* of relaxing the stutter response, PRACTICE USING THE ADDED STRETCH IN ALL OF THE ABOVE SITUATIONS.

I cannot stress too strongly the importance of being aware of, and *experiencing the relaxation of the stutter response.* That's the whole idea. That's how the techniques work. *When you relax the stutter response, you gain control of your speech.*

PRACTICE BOTH OF THESE STRETCHES
EVERY DAY, SEVERAL TIMES PER DAY,
IN DIFFERENT SITUATIONS.

USING THE CHERI J. STRETCHES
IN THE REAL WORLD

As you find other situations in which to practice, you will start noticing that you actually use the Stretch and the Added Stretch, not as practice per se, but as truly needed in real-life speaking situations. YOU JUST WILL. YOU WILL BECAUSE THEY WORK. It's really quite exciting.

As you begin to use the stretches in real-life situations, they still might sound contrived and VERY obvious to you, but in actuality, they will sound natural to the listener, as I mentioned earlier. It's amazing. Both stretches truly blend into your regular speech inflections.

It probably will take a while to feel comfortable using the stretches. You WILL eventually get comfortable with them, especially after you see how slick they work.

As you experience using the Stretch and the Added Stretch in a few real-life situations, take notice as you begin to gain control of your speech. It is very exciting and empowering! You will want to branch out to more and more situations. As you do so, you will become more proficient. THE MORE OFTEN YOU USE THE STRETCHES, THE BETTER YOU GET AT IT, AND THE BETTER YOU GET AT IT, THE MORE OFTEN YOU WILL WANT TO USE THEM. IT'S A LIFE CHANGING CYCLE.

You will need to REMAIN MINDFUL, in order to REMEMBER to use the Stretch and the Added Stretch, especially during the first year or so. When I first started using the Stretch (I had not come up with the Added Stretch, yet) I often would forget to use it and would stumble on with my stuttering. Since I worked with students who stuttered, my sessions with them would help me get back on track and stay mindful. Perhaps you could put notes in special places so that you remember to use the Stretches.

Very possibly, you will find the Stretches easier to use in some situations than in others, and when you are well rested. As with all or most fluency techniques, the Cheri J. Stretch and its companion, the Cheri J. Added Stretch may not work 100% of the time, but the combination, after lots and lots of practice, really works. Just, remember, Rome was not built in a day—or weeks—or months. It takes time. *My deepest hope for you is that you will work at it, and that the Stretches will work for you most of the time and eventually become a natural part of your speech.*

With the combination of the Stretch and the Added Stretch, some of you may eventually acquire complete fluency. It does not matter how much of it is controlled fluency. Fluency is fluency.

Some of you will not be as fluent as you would like. Possibly, you have not given it enough time and practice. Just maybe your expectations are too high. Remember, complete fluency would be great, but it is not the goal. The goal is to gain enough stutter control to achieve greater confidence in one's speaking and in one's self.

It took three years for the Stretch to become a natural part of my speaking pattern. During that time, the percentage of my stuttering reduced significantly.

After recently including the Added Stretch to my communication, I have even more control of my speech. I'm not totally fluent, but darn close. I still have my moments, but because of the fluency and control that I have gained, I am no longer afraid to speak in any situation.

THE STRETCH AND THE ADDED STRETCH WORK FOR ME MOST OF THE TIME AND HAVE CHANGED MY LIFE FOREVER.

VERY SEVERE STUTTERING

IF YOUR STUTTERING IS TOO SEVERE TO USE THE CHERI J. STRETCH TECHNIQUE RIGHT AWAY, you will need to experience fluency in a different manner, though it is a temporary step. I believe that *CHORAL READING*, i.e. *reading aloud, in unison with another person,* could be that step.

Choral reading distracts the brain and you are able to read without stuttering. However, in order for this to make a difference, it will need to be done on a regular basis—RELIGIOUSLY—even if you are not religious!

Find a person whom you trust, who is willing to spend the time with you. Read aloud, in unison, for at least an hour at a time, per day. Read more than once a day, if possible. Pay attention to your speech while reading, and *notice your fluency. Feel it.* Record some of your reading, so that you can listen to yourself and truly be aware of your fluency. *Know that you can be fluent.*

After you have been choral reading for about two weeks or so, begin practicing the Stretch technique in privacy. Practice using the Stretch while talking to your dog, cat, baby, plants, even though you generally do not stutter during these times. I know. It is an interesting phenomenon.

When you feel that you are ready, use the Cheri J. Stretch in one, non-threatening real-life situation. (Combine it with the Schwartz Airflow Technique, if you find that helpful.) If you are successful, truly acknowledge it. Feel the joy. Then practice in another situation. Keep going, and going.

If you are not successful when you first attempt to use the Stretch (or the Schwartz Airflow) in a real-life situation, please don't give up. Please, keep practicing and practicing with your plants or pet, then have a go at it again and again. Be the Energizer Bunny.

After you become successful with the Stretch and/or the Schwartz Air Flow Technique in a few situations, pay close attention to the *relaxation of the stutter response.* Truly *feel* it. Know that it happened. Continue to use it in as many situations as you can. For all people who stutter, *it is extremely important to frequently experience the relaxation of the stutter response.* This will give you the courage to go on.

AFTER YOU HAVE HAD SUCCESS WITH THE STRETCH, START USING THE *ADDED STRETCH*. Use it frequently, but only in comfortable, safe situations at first. Pay attention, and *feel the relaxation of the stutter response,* as you do with the Stretch. As you become more fluent this way, you will be ready to use both stretches in more situations. I believe you will find success with the combination of these two stretches.

REMEMBER, ALL OF THIS TAKES A LOT OF COURAGE AND PERSISTENCE, AS WELL AS PRACTICE AND TIME.

IN CLOSING

My dear readers, this is your life. Please, give the Cheri J. Stretch and its companion the Cheri J. Added Stretch your best shot. Be your own champion, your own hero. You can do it!

To be in control of one's speech can have a huge, positive impact on one's life. I am a different person now, due to my fluency. For the most part, I have no avoidance of words, people or situations. My fluency has given me confidence in speaking, thus confidence in myself. It has given me the freedom to speak wherever and whenever I choose. It has given me a new lease on life!

The Cheri J. Stretch and the Cheri J. Added Stretch Techniques for fluency offered me the **FREEDOM**

To do!

To be!

To live!

**THIS IS MY GIFT TO YOU,
MY DEAR READERS.**

**Respectfully,
Cheri Jensen**

Please feel free to email me with questions, concerns
or comments.

cherilynn@q.com

* cherilynn.jensen@gmail.com

References

Guitar, Barry: An Integrated Approach
To Its Nature And Treatment,
Second Edition (1999) Stuttering Foundation of America,
P.O. box 11749
Memphis, TN 38111-0749

Jezer, Marty: Stuttering: A Life Bound up
In Words (1997), Basic Books
10 East 53rd Street
New York, NY 10022-5299`

Van Riper, Charles: Speech Correction: Principles and
Methods (4th ed.) (1963) Inglewood Cliffs, NJ:
Prentice-Hall

Schwartz, Martin: Stutter No More (Airflow Technique)